ISBN 978 1 938068 31 7

Library of Congress Control Number: 2018953568

Published by Oxvision Books
4001 Tamiami Trail North, Suite 250, Naples, FL 34103

Find us at: oxvisionmedia.com & liliastrotter.com

TURN YOUR EYES UPON JESUS

A Story and a Song

ARTIST
Tim Ladwig

AUTHOR
Miriam Huffman Rockness

PUBLISHED BY
OXVISION
BOOKS

Have you ever wondered
how a song comes into being?
Which comes first?
The words or the music?
How is a song presented to the world?

This is a story about two people and one song. It is the account
of two women, each remarkable in her own right, and how their
unique talents merged to create one of the most beloved songs of
the 19th century which has endured to this day:
"Turn Your Eyes upon Jesus."

It is worth noting that while these women had much in common,
they never met each other. But their talent and their faithfulness
to their Master would bring their very souls together
in a way one could never calculate.

The Story
LILIAS TROTTER

Born in 1853 into the wealthy family of Alexander and Isabela Trotter, Lilias grew up in the privileged surrounds of London's fashionable West End near Regent's Park during the Golden Age of Queen Victoria. She was privately tutored by governesses at home. She enjoyed travel in Europe—by coach and rail—during the summer months. Her almost idyllic childhood ended when, at the age of 12, she experienced the death of her beloved father. To whom did she then turn? To her heavenly Father.

Her spiritual responsiveness was quickened in her early-twenties during the Moody/Sankey Revival meetings. She sang in the choir and helped in the Inquiry room following the services. She also participated in the deeper life conferences held at Broadlands, Oxford and Brighton that developed into the permanent Keswick Convention, a world-wide institution vital to this day. Her freshly kindled faith prompted her to serve in missions work with prostitutes at Victoria Station and, eventually,

as a full-time volunteer with the YWCA at their Hostel at Welbeck Street, setting up the first public restaurants for working women.

Alongside her enthusiasm for service was a passion for art. She seemed to be born with an innate sensitivity to beauty, matched by an exceptional God-given artistic talent. This talent, and the place it would have in her life, was profoundly put to the test by her meeting in Venice, in 1876, with John Ruskin, the most important art critic of the day. After seeing some of her sketches, Ruskin was captivated by this young talent. He took Lilias on sketching expeditions and introduced her to the artistic wonders along the Grand Canal.

Their friendship developed from there. She spent vacations at Brantwood, his Lake District home in Coniston—where he continued to mentor her in art—and through their correspondence. His ambitions for her were great: he believed that under his tutelage she could become one of England's greatest living artists.

But Lilias, already deeply involved in ministry in London, realized that a choice would be required of her. Ruskin taunted her with letters indicating his frustration with her growing passion for the poor in London— and its effect on their relationship: "Am I not bad enough? Am I not good enough? Am I not whatever it is enough to be looked after a little when I'm ill, as well as those blessed Magdalenes?"

The role of art in her life was brought to the test, May 1879, at the age of 26, during a two-week visit to Brantwood—a challenge she anticipated in a letter to a close friend: "I shall probably go to see Mr. Ruskin for a few days, which I rather dread. I see as clear as daylight now, I cannot give myself to painting in the way he means and continue to seek first the kingdom of God and His righteousness."

With this painful issue of the heart resolved at last, she threw herself into her city work with an undivided heart. She continued her friendship with Ruskin. She continued to paint. But her first priority was to her ministry at Welbeck Street Institute, from where she fully intended to love the needy in London for the rest of her life.

Then, almost a decade later, in May 1887, at age 34, in a meeting for missions at Welbeck Street Institute, she heard a message about those in Algeria who had never heard the gospel of Christ, and she felt the call of God on her life to go to North Africa. The rest happened in an astonishingly short period of time. The following March she set off with two friends for Algiers where she knew no one, and where she knew not a word of Arabic, the native language. Her initial enthusiasm for the exotic land was captured in a pocket sketchbook—images that would have delighted the color-loving Ruskin! She spent the remaining 40 years of her life in the French colony bringing the light and life and love of Jesus to the Arab Muslim people. She learned the language and loved the people, taking up residence in the Arab section of the Casbah or the fortified ancient city—in essence, the slum area of Algiers.

From her base in Algiers, over the next four decades, as others came alongside her, she set up stations along the coast of North Africa and deeper down into the Sahara. In the early decades she scouted by camel areas rarely visited by Europeans—much less a European woman—developing a profound and rare relationship with the Sufi Mystic Brotherhood. She even wrote a treasured book for them: *The Sevenfold Secret*. She died in 1928—at age 75—leaving a team of workers united under the name Algiers Mission Band, which merged forty-some years later with North African Mission—later to be re-named Arab World Ministries as their mission broadened beyond North Africa.

The Song
HELEN LEMMEL

H elen Lemmel, born a decade later than Lilias, in 1863, had much in common with her. She was born in England, but of modest means, her father being a Wesleyan Methodist pastor. The most dramatic experience of her childhood came in 1876 when she was 12: Her family sailed to the United States in a steamboat, where they lived briefly in Mississippi before settling in Wisconsin.

She, like Lilias, was artistically gifted from a young age, but in a different field—music. And she liked to write. She gained a reputation as a brilliant singer. As a young woman she traveled widely throughout the Midwest giving concerts in many churches.

In 1904, at the age of 40, she moved to Seattle, Washington. Here she was able to merge her remarkable literary abilities with her love of music. She became music critic for the *Seattle-Post Intelligencer*. While interviewing the noted singer Ernestine Shumann-Hein, Helen heard and then heeded Ernestine's advice: to advance her vocal studies in Germany.

She moved to Germany in 1907 where she spent the next four years continuing her study of voice with private lessons. While in Germany, she met and married a wealthy European.

Upon the completion of her studies, she moved back to the Midwest [1911]. Throughout the United States, she gave concerts in churches and traveled on the Chautauqua circuit, a popular performance venue of that era. She was greatly in demand across the country, performing her own patriotic compositions for soldiers in Military Camps and providing programs of her own stories and songs of a wide range of subjects.

Even as she experienced success in secular venues, her first love and loyalty was to her Christian faith. She continued to give concerts in churches and eventually became the vocal music teacher at the Moody Bible Institute in Chicago, even leading a women's choral group for Billy Sunday during the peak of his career.

She continued her literary pursuits, writing hymns as well as stories and poems for children. Her book for children, *Story of the Bible*, was met with wide acclaim.

Then a tragedy struck that would have a life-altering effect. She was diagnosed with an affliction that would result in blindness. Her husband, unable to cope with that reality, abandoned the marriage, leaving her to cope on her own. What might have been a debilitating experience, physically as well as emotionally, only turned her more completely to God and to her most compelling vocation: the composing of hymns from the depths of her heart and life experience. She authored around 500 hymns, lyrics and music, many still in circulation.

She moved back to Seattle, upon retirement. Living in reduced circumstances, she continued to write out her soul in poems set to music. Now, totally blind, she would pick out the notes on a small plastic keyboard and call upon friends to record them before she forgot them.

When asked "How are you?" her frequent reply was, *"I am fine in the things that count."* Like Lilias she continued to write until the end of her life. She died at 97 years of age, anticipating in advance, *"...God is going to bless me with a great heavenly keyboard. I can hardly wait!"*

The Song
TURN YOUR EYES UPON JESUS

How then did collaboration between Lilias Trotter and Helen Lemmel take place? How did one song merge from two women who never met each other?

The story of the song begins in 1901. Lilias had had a very busy and exhausting year in Algiers. Bidding her teary-eyed Arab friends a tender farewell, she boarded a ship for the Continent where she anticipated a much needed respite, in Switzerland, from the heat and the labor of North Africa. After several days in Berne, she and several friends secured lodging at the head of a nearby valley resplendent with crowds of meadow flowers accented by the snow crests above. Noting that she was "still in the state of mental fatigue which is the first stage of resting," she sought out a quiet place to be alone with God.

While in a place of solitude, she recorded this observation in her diary for July 23:

> The word of the Lord came to me this morning through a dandeli-on. It was early morning and I was sitting in a little wood near the Hotel. The sun was climbing behind a steep cliff to the east, and its light was flooding from a dark corner of purple brown stems & tawny moss, there shown out a great golden star. It was just a dandelion, & half-withered—but it was full face to the sun, & had caught into its heart all the glory it could hold, & was shining so radiantly that the dew that lay on it still, made a perfect aureole round its head.

She proceeded to move from the world of the seen to the invisible truths to which it pointed: "Gathered up—focussed lives—intent with the intentions of the one aim—Christ—those are the lives on which God can concentrate blessedness. It is all for all."

Later she elaborated on this lesson from nature with parallel spiritual truths and published it in a little leaflet, "Focussed." Noting the unvarying laws that govern the material universe, she observed the same in the laws of the spirit: as with the law of optics, for example, when one focuses on one object, the other objects fade. Offering a series of questions to help determine what is the focus of our lives, she concluded with this chal-lenge: "Turn full your soul's vision to Jesus, and look and look at Him, and a strange dimness will come over all that is apart from Him, and the Divine 'attrait' by which God's saints are made, even in this 20th century will lay hold of you. For 'He is worthy' to have all there is to be had in the heart that He has died to win."

"Focussed" enjoyed a modest circulation among Lilias's friends and the supporters of her mission. Most likely, that would have been the end of the story if this little leaflet had not been given to Helen Lemmel by a missionary friend in the United States. It contained a statement that had profound impact on her: "So then, turn your eyes upon Him, look full into His face and you will find that the things of earth will acquire a strange new dimness." The rest is best told in Helen's own words: "I stood still and singing in my soul and spirit was the chorus, with no one conscious moment of putting word to word to make rhyme or note to note to make melody:

Turn your eyes upon Jesus,
Look full in His wonderful face,
And the things of earth will grow strangely dim,
In the light of His glory and grace.

THE HE...

With Expression. (S.C.T.B...)

Focussed

A Story + a Song.

light for a look at the Sa-viour, And...
us sin no more hath do...ion— For...
go to a world that is...ing, His...

Helen's new hymn was first published in London, England, 1918, in the form of a pamphlet. Four years later it was included in a collection of sixty-seven of Helen's songs, *Glad Songs*, the hymnal for the Keswick Convention—Lilias's early formative spiritual influence. Here it was received with much enthusiasm, becoming the theme song for the Keswick Convention.

But that is not the end of the story. When Lilias learned of this song based on her little leaflet, she was bedridden in Algeria. That did not stop this visionary woman from reworking the original, simple leaflet into a lovely new edition. Several years later (1926), this revised leaflet, "Focussed: A Story & a Song," was printed on ivory stock and bound by a slender cord. The cover featured a pen and ink drawing of a fir wood with the tiny flash of dandelion shining from the ground. It ended with the entire text and musical score of Helen Lemmel's song—bringing together, at last, the talents of these two remarkable women.

Since then, "Turn Your Eyes upon Jesus" has been widely received throughout the Christian church, included in countless hymnals and recorded by musicians to this day. And is it not remarkable that Helen Lemmel, the nearly blind woman who illuminated the concept of looking full into the wonderful face of Jesus, was inspired by Lilias Trotter, who spent a lifetime gleaning invisible realities from visible manifestation? From the seen to the unseen... from the physical to the spiritual. So we fix our eyes not on what is seen, but on what is unseen.

> For what is seen is temporary, but what is unseen is eternal.
> *–2 Corinthians 4:18 NIV*

> Let us fix our eyes upon Jesus, the author and finisher of our faith...
> *–Hebrews 12:2*

On the follwing pages: the cover of "Focussed" drawn by Lilias Trotter, her lesson from the sunlit dandelion in an Alpine meadow, and the song "The Heavenly Vision" (now known by the title "Turn Your Eyes upon Jesus") by Helen Lemmel.

Focussed

A Story + a Song.

It was in a little wood in early morning. The sun was climbing behind a steep cliff in the east, and its light was flooding nearer and nearer and then making pools among the trees. Suddenly, from a dark corner of purple brown stems and tawny moss, there shone out a great golden star. It was full face to the sun, and had caught into its heart all the glory it could hold, and was shining so radiantly that the dew that lay on it still made a perfect aureole round its head. And it seemed to talk, standing there—to talk about the possibility of making the very best of these lives of ours.

For if the Sun of Righteousness has risen upon our hearts, there is an ocean of grace and love and power lying all around us, an ocean to which all earthly light is but a drop, and it is ready to transfigure us, as the sunshine transfigured the dandelion, and on the same condition—that we stand full face to God.

Gathered up, *focussed* lives, intent on one aim—Christ—these are the lives on which God can concentrate blessedness. It is "all for all" by a law as unvarying as any law that governs the material universe.

We see the principle shadowed in the trend of science; the telephone and the wireless in the realm of sound, the use of radium and the ultra violet rays in the realm of light. All these work by gathering into focus currents and waves that, dispersed, cannot serve us. In every branch of learning and workmanship the tendency of these days is to specialize—to take up one point and follow it to the uttermost.

And Satan knows well the power of concentration; if a soul is likely to get under the sway of the inspiration, "this one thing I do," he will turn all his energies to bring in side interests that will shatter the gathering intensity.

And they lie all around, these interests. Never has it been so easy to live in half a dozen good harmless worlds at once—art, music, social-science, games, motoring, the following of some profession, and so on. And between them we run the risk of drifting about, the "good" hiding the "best" even more effectually than it could be hidden by downright frivolity with its smothered heart-ache at its own emptiness.

It is easy to find out whether our lives are focussed, and if so, where the focus lies. Where do our thoughts settle when consciousness comes in the morning? Where do they swing back when the pressure is off during the day? Does this test not give the clue? Then dare to have it out with God— and after all, that is the shortest way. Dare to lay bare your whole life and being before Him, and ask Him to show you whether or not all is focussed on Christ and His glory. Dare to face the fact that unfocussed, good and useful as it may seem, it will prove to have failed of its purpose.

What does this focusing mean? Study the matter and you will see that it means two things—gathering in all that can be gathered, and letting the rest drop. The working of any lens—microscope, telescope, camera—will show you this: the lens of your own eye, in the room where you are sitting, as clearly as any other. Look at the window bars, and the beyond is only a shadow; look through at the distance and it is the bars that turn into ghosts. You have to choose which you will fix your gaze upon and let the other go.

Are we ready for a cleavage to be wrought through the whole range of our lives, like the division long ago at the taking of Jericho, the division between things that could be passed through the fire of consecration into "the treasury of the Lord," and the things that, unable to "abide the fire," must be destroyed? All aims, all ambitions, all desires, all pursuits—shall we dare to drop them if they cannot be gathered sharply and clearly into the focus of "this one thing I do"?

Will it not make life narrow, this focusing? In a sense, it will—just as the mountain path grows narrower, for it matters more and more, the higher we go, where we set our feet—but there is always, as it narrows, a wider and wider outlook, and purer, clearer air. Narrow as Christ's life was narrow, this is our aim; narrow as regards self-seeking, broad as the love of God to all around. Is there anything to fear in that?

And in the narrowing and focusing, the channel will be prepared for God's power—like the stream hemmed between the rock-beds, that wells up in a spring—like the burning glass that gathers the rays into an intensity that will kindle fire. It is worth while to let God see what He can do with these lives of ours, when "to live is Christ."

Turn full your soul's vision to Jesus, and look and look at Him, and strange dimness will come over all that is apart from Him, even in this 20th century, will lay hold of you. For "He is worthy" to have all there is to be had in the heart that He has died to win.

> Hath not each heart a passion and a dream,
> Each some companionship for ever sweet,
> And each in saddest skies some silver gleam,
> And each some passing joy, too fair and fleet,
> And each a staff and stay, though frail it prove,
> And each a face he fain would ever see?
>
> And what have I? an endless stream of love,
> A rapture, and a glory, and a calm,
> A life that is an everlasting Psalm,
> All, O Beloved, in Thee.
> —*Tersteegen.*

THE HEA

With Expression. (S.C.T.B)

1. O soul, are you weary and tr
2. Thro' death in-to life ev-er-la
3. His word shall not fail you—He p

light for a look at the Sa
us sin no more hath domin
go to a world that is dy

Copyright, 1922, by H. H. L

THE HEAVENLY VISION.

VISION.

by HELEN HOWARTH LEMMEL.

t in the darkness you see? There's
d, and we fol-low Him there Over
Him, and all will be well: Then

re a-bun-dant and free!
an conquer'rs we are!
t sal-va-tion to tell!

REFRAIN

Turn your eyes up-on Je - sus, Look full in His wonder-ful face;..........

......And the things of earth will grow strangely dim In the light of His glory and grace.

Follow
GRANDPA
on his many adventures...

Find these books and others at oxvisionmedia.com or your favorite online retailer.

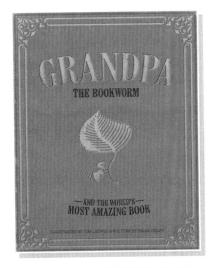

GRANDPA THE BOOKWORM AND THE WORLD'S MOST AMAZING BOOK

GRANDPA, HOW BIG IS YOUR LOVE?

GRANDPA'S DIET

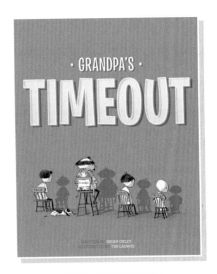

GRANDPA'S TIMEOUT

GRANDPA SAVES THE DAY

GRANDPA'S OVERALLS

More Oxvision Books
for Young Readers

GRANDPA, THE MUSIC EXECUTIVE

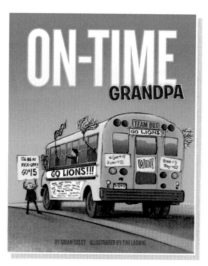

ON-TIME GRANDPA

LILY: THE GIRL WHO COULD SEE

**W.S. "FLUKE" HOLLAND:
THE FATHER OF THE DRUMS**

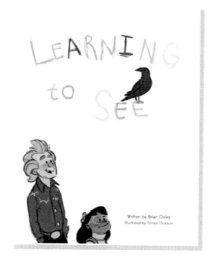

LEARNING TO SEE

OXVISION
BOOKS